Contents

Introduction	2
The Queen's Silver Jubilee	4
Working at Waterloo…	7
…and down the line to Clapham	13
The Great Northern route from King's Cross	16
Derailment at Clink Road Junction	19
On the Isle of Wight	22
Catch it while you can: 'The Corkscrew Shuttle'	26
West from Paddington	28
London's Underground	32
Down in Dorset	39
Around Worcester	42
Southern serendipity	44
1977 Happenings (1)	6
1977 Happenings (2)	30
1977 Arrivals & Departures	16
TV favourites	37
No1 records	41

Silver Link Publishing Ltd
The Trundle
Ringstead Road
Great Addington
Kettering
Northants NN14 4BW

Tel/Fax: 01536 330588
email: sales@nostalgiacollection.com
Website: www.nostalgiacollection.com

Printed and bound in the Czech Republic

© Chris Harris 2014
Photographs by Ray Ruffell © *The NOSTALGIA Collection* archive, unless otherwise credited

All rights reserved. No part of this publication may be reproduced, stored in a retrieval system or transmitted, in any form or by any means, electronic, mechanical, photocopying, recording or otherwise, without prior permission in writing from Silver Link Publishing Ltd.

First published in 2014

British Library Cataloguing in Publication Data
A catalogue record for this book is available from the British Library.

ISBN 978 1 85794 435 8

Frontispiece: **PORTSMOUTH HARBOUR**
This station is very aptly named as it is located right on the waterfront, giving passengers direct access to the ferries to the Isle of Wight. Excursion trains are occupying Platforms 2 and 3 on Sunday 31 July 1977; that at Platform 2 on the left, with Class 47 diesel-electric locomotive No 47514 resting by the buffer stops, will depart at 1848 for Taunton via Bristol Temple Meads and Weston-super-Mare, while that at Platform 3 will leave at 1915 for Alfreton & Mansfield Parkway via Burton-upon-Trent and Derby. Note the helpful chalk boards telling the returning excursionists when they will be able to board their trains prior to departure.

Introduction
Silver Jubilee year

Her Majesty Queen Elizabeth II had become monarch of the United Kingdom on 6 February 1952 following the death of her father, King George VI. The main Silver Jubilee celebrations in 1977 took place during the summer months. The Queen extensively toured the UK and also visited many Commonwealth countries, and the celebrations came to a climax on the evening of Monday 6 June when the Queen lit a beacon at Windsor, which started a chain of such beacons across the country. The following morning there was a Service of Thanksgiving in St Paul's Cathedral, while during the afternoon people throughout the land held street parties and village parties, which were much enjoyed despite the weather being unseasonably cool and (at times) damp. The monarchy enjoyed a surge of popularity, although a very small section of the pop music scene took a contrary view; punk rock group the Sex Pistols released a record called *God Save the Queen* that bore no resemblance to the National Anthem.

    Tennis fans had further cause for celebration that summer when Virginia Wade won the Women's Singles Championship at Wimbledon.

    In 1977 more than 26% of the UK workforce was employed in the manufacturing sector (at the time of writing it is nearer 8%), but it was a time of considerable industrial

Introduction

unrest. British Leyland's car manufacturing plant at Longbridge was notorious for strike action, and there were clashes between pickets and police at the Grunwick film processing laboratory. The service sector was also affected; in November and December the country faced the first ever national strike by firemen, who were seeking a 30% wage rise. Emergency cover was provided by troops using old Civil Defence 'Green Goddess' fire engines that dated from the 1950s. Among the more unusual groups to take industrial action were undertakers, who came out on strike in London during October. Meanwhile the Government had lost its majority in the House of Commons, but Prime Minister James Callaghan had formed an agreement with Liberal Leader David Steel (the 'Lib-Lab Pact'), which meant that the Government had survived a vote of no confidence in March (and indeed subsequently remained in power until 1979).

Amid great publicity, Freddie Laker launched his 'Skytrain' in September, offering a single fare of just £59 from Gatwick to New York; the standard price at that time was £186. Two months later, at the premium end of the air travel market, British Airways inaugurated its regular London to New York supersonic Concorde service in November. And getting from central London to Heathrow became easier from December 1977 when the Queen opened an extension of the Underground's Piccadilly Line from Hatton Cross (reached in 1975) onwards to Heathrow Central. Sadly 1977 also saw the worst tragedy in the history of air travel: 583 people lost their lives when two Boeing 747 jumbo jets, operated by Pan American and KLM, collided on the runway at Los Rodeos airport, Tenerife, on Sunday 27 March.

1977 was the first year that sales of foreign cars outstripped those of British cars on the home market; car ownership was increasing, with more than 55% of UK households owning one or more cars (at the time of writing the figure is 75%). A White Paper in June 1977 looked at future policy on rail services, but given its somewhat precarious position in the House of Commons the Government did not seek to legislate any possibly controversial transport measures at this time.

At the cinema in December *Star Wars* opened in the UK; it had already proved a massive hit in the USA and was quickly equally popular with British audiences. Perhaps slightly less known is a bizarre incident that had taken place a few weeks previously. On Saturday 26 November viewers who received ITV's Southern Television from the Hannington transmitter in Hampshire were watching the early evening news when suddenly the voice of the newsreader was drowned by a deep masculine voice, accompanied by severe static, which purported to be from another galaxy and indicated that it was imperative that the inhabitants of earth laid down their weapons of war and learned to live together in peace. The voice spoke for some minutes until normal transmission was restored. It was later explained that hoaxers had jammed the signal at the Hannington transmitter, but those responsible for the prank have never been apprehended.

Although inflation was dropping slowly, it still averaged 15.8% through the year, making 1977 the fourth consecutive year to have an inflation rate in double figures. And as well as buying less, the 'pound in your pocket' also became slightly smaller with the introduction of a new, more compact pound note from 23 August.

Let us remember a year when there were just three television channels to chose from (although most people had now acquired colour TV), while home computers, CDs and DVDs were all some way into the future. The Silver Jubilee gave us all something to celebrate, and the overriding memory is of an enjoyable year despite a summer that was nothing like as warm and sunny as the previous one; in general people were happy to put aside other problems and have fun. So let us re-visit 1977…

Chris Harris, Poole, Dorset

The Queen's Silver Jubilee

Workshops organisation, and started trading from 1 January 1970.

International Harvesters had established a presence in Doncaster during the 1930s, but owing to its premises being requisitioned in the Second World War, the manufacture of tractors started in 1949. Production was to continue until 2007 when the factory, by then owned by an Italian parent company – Argo – was closed.

DONCASTER In 1977 we celebrated the Silver Jubilee of Her Majesty Queen Elizabeth II. The country was delighted to commemorate this achievement, which had not been reached by the two previous monarchs; the Queen's uncle, King Edward VIII, had abdicated after less than a year, while her father, King George VI, sadly died after just 15 years as sovereign. Large numbers of people turned out to see the Queen as she undertook a tour around Britain during the Jubilee year, and many companies also celebrated the historic event. Ray Ruffell photographed this patriotic lineside sign, jointly sponsored by British Rail Engineering and International Harvesters, from a passing train at Doncaster on Wednesday 26 October 1977.

The Great Northern Railway had established a works at Doncaster in 1853; known to local railwaymen as 'The Plant', many thousands of locomotives and carriages were built there – including such icons as *Mallard* and *Flying Scotsman*. The 1968 Transport Act had included a provision that allowed the (then) nationalised railway workshops to manufacture for other undertakings; previously this had been prohibited. As a result British Rail Engineering Limited had been set up in late 1969 in place of the former British Railways

WATERLOO The week commencing Sunday 5 June 1977 was designated as Jubilee Week, the Monday and the Tuesday both being granted as public holidays. During that week Ray Ruffell was 'flying the flag' for the Jubilee by displaying this small Union Jack pennant in the window of his van while working as a guard on British Rail's Southern Region. This photograph was taken on a suburban working approaching London Waterloo.

The Queen's Silver Jubilee

PORTSMOUTH HARBOUR The Queen's Silver Jubilee Fleet Review was held at Spithead on Tuesday 28 June 1977, and Her Majesty travelled to Portsmouth by special train the previous day. Given the pomp of the occasion, it is perhaps surprising that the Royal Train stock was not used, but on this occasion the Queen's special train was made up of 4BEP electric multiple unit No 7020. This was one of the four-car buffet units built in 1961 for the second phase of the Kent Coast electrification scheme; it is clearly in sparkling condition, and these units were very spacious and comfortable in their original form. The special train was scheduled to arrive at Portsmouth Harbour station at 1740 on Monday 27 June, when the Queen was received by the Lord Lieutenant of Hampshire (The Right Honourable Earl

of Malmesbury TD), the Lord Mayor of Portsmouth (Councillor George Austin), and the Commander in Chief, Naval Home Command (Admiral Sir David Williams KCB, ADC). Brian Jackson took these photographs after the Royal party had proceeded to the South Railway Jetty and the train was waiting to depart from the station as empty stock. *Brian Jackson*

PORTSMOUTH To handle the crowds expected to come to Portsmouth for the Fleet Review, motorists were directed to out-of-town parking areas and a park-and-ride system was operated. A number of buses were brought in from various companies for this, including several that had been painted in the official Silver Jubilee livery. Leading this group of buses waiting for returning passengers near South Parade Pier are East Kent Road Car Company Leyland AN68/ECW registration JJG 12P, Potteries Motor Traction Company Bristol VRT/ECW fleet number 652, and Eastern National Bristol VRT/ECW fleet number SD 3053. *Brian Jackson*

1977 Happenings (1)

January
- Home Secretary Roy Jenkins announces he will be leaving House of Commons to become President of European Commission.

February
- Foreign Secretary Anthony Crosland dies after suffering a stroke.
- David Owen becomes Foreign Secretary.

March
- Government indicates that inflation has pushed up prices by almost 70% during the past three years.
- British Leyland announces intent to dismiss striking toolmakers at the company's Longbridge plant in Birmingham.
- Government wins vote of no confidence in House of Commons after Prime Minister James Callaghan makes deal with Liberal leader David Steel.
- Budget reduces income tax from 35p in the pound to 33p in the pound.

April
- British Aerospace formed to oversee nationalised aviation industry.

May
- Her Majesty the Queen launches HMS *Invincible* at Barrow-in-Furness.
- Silver Jubilee review of police at Hendon.
- Silver Jubilee Air Fair at Biggin Hill.
- Her Majesty the Queen starts Silver Jubilee tour of United Kingdom in Scotland, and opens new terminal building at Edinburgh Airport.
- M5 motorway is completed with opening of final stretch near Exeter by Prime Minister James Callaghan.

June
- Jubilee celebrations held throughout the United Kingdom to celebrate 25 years of Queen's reign. Tuesday 7 June is granted as additional public holiday and, although weather is generally cool and damp, street parties and other celebrations are much enjoyed.

Waterloo station. These staff rooms were linked by a gallery on the platform side, which gave an excellent view across the station, as this photograph taken on Monday 28 February 1977 shows. A variety of rolling stock, including 4SUB, 4VEP, 2HAP and 4REP units, can be seen. Notice also the temporary wooden ticket collectors' huts; these are seen again from platform level in the second photograph, also taken on 27 February. A new barrier line, incorporating a number of shops and kiosks, was in the course of construction, replacing the previous Bostwick-style gates that had dated back to Southern Railway days. This work was completed in the autumn of 1977.

Working at Waterloo...

WATERLOO was the last London terminus to be served by steam trains, which remained on main-line services here until the completion of the Bournemouth electrification scheme in July 1967. One consequence of this electrification was the closure of Nine Elms locomotive depot; to replace the main-line booking-on point that was previously at the depot, some staff accommodation was constructed over the barrier ends of Platforms 1-6 at

WATERLOO The first station on this site opened in 1848 as Waterloo Bridge; the present title came into use in 1882. The station grew in a rather piecemeal fashion over the next 40 years, and was something of a confused muddle by the end of the 19th century.

This was gently satirised in Jerome K. Jerome's delightful book *Three Men in a Boat*, published in 1889, but in reality the confusion caused to intending passengers by the bewildering layout was not a joke and the station became the subject of serious press criticism. In 1898 the London & South Western Railway decided to demolish the entire collection of bits and replace them with a modern purpose-built terminus. Work proceeded through the early years of the 20th century; a change to the initial plans was the retention of the 1885 'North' station, which was fully integrated into the new concourse, but retained the original roof over the platforms. The completed station was officially opened by Her Majesty Queen Mary on 21 March 1922. A commendable feature of the rebuilt station was the provision of very clear mechanical departure boards between Platforms 6 and 7 and between Platforms 18 and 19. This simple, robust technology lasted until 1977, when the LSWR departure boards were replaced by a large Solari departure indicator located above Platforms 12-15; linked to the same system were small departure indicators by the stairways giving access to the platforms from the underground station subway. The new train indicator control office was photographed on Friday 4 November 1977; as can be seen in the second photograph, CCTV had also been provided, enabling staff to view the platforms.

Working at Waterloo...

much of the 1970s sets of British Railways Standard Mark 1 carriages were used, the later Mark 2 stock not being cascaded onto the line until 1978-79. The formation of the 1300 Waterloo to Exeter train on Wednesday 5 October 1977 was therefore something of a portent of things to come. The train is headed by Class 47 diesel-electric locomotive No 47111, which had entered traffic in December 1963 as D1699, and which remained in service with British Rail until February 1986; at the time of this photograph it was allocated to Bristol Bath Road shed. The train is formed of Mark 2 stock; the carriage nearest the locomotive is a Mark 2b with wider end doors, while the side corridor 1st and the Open 2nd seen in the second photograph of are the earlier Mark 2a type, with the Open 2nd on the extreme left again being a Mark 2b.

WATERLOO Although the majority of trains from London Waterloo were operated by electric multiple units by 1977, one route on which locomotive haulage did remain was the line to Exeter via Salisbury and Yeovil Junction. Operated by steam until 1964, Western Region diesel-hydraulic 'Warship' Class locomotives then provided the motive power until they were replaced by Class 33 diesel-electric locomotives in October 1971. This reduction in power was regretted by many regular users of the service, although it has to be said that the Class 33s had a better reputation for reliability than the 'Warships'. The Class 33s were the staple motive power until 1990, when Class 50 diesel-electrics were allocated to the route. For

WATERLOO In 1977 Southern Region suburban services were in the hands of traditional electric multiple units with a slam door to each compartment or seating bay, as exemplified by this scene at Waterloo on Monday 28 February. On the left, BR Standard 2EPB unit No 5790 has arrived with a terminating service, while in the centre of the photograph 4SUB unit No 4680 will form the next departure for Effingham Junction. Entering traffic in July 1950, No 4680 was in service for 33 years, being withdrawn in July 1983. On the far right of the photograph, 4SUB unit No 4638 heads a train waiting to depart from Platform 1 for the Kingston loop via Wimbledon. This unit was new in September 1949 and was withdrawn from service in June 1981.

Working at Waterloo...

WATERLOO Taken from Waterloo signal box on Friday 25 February, this photograph illustrates the difference in height between the old 'North' station dating from 1885 and the rest of the rebuilt terminus (see also page 8). The retained 1885 station was used by services to and from the Reading and Windsor lines. As well as the 4CIG unit awaiting departure, stock can be seen stabled in Waterloo North Sidings. This is a scene that was to alter very considerably in the early 1990s, when the old 1885 station and the North Sidings were swept away to make room for the Waterloo Eurostar terminus.

Below: **WATERLOO** For many years a landmark beside the north side of the tracks at the entrance to Waterloo station, a very 1930s-style concrete signal box was brought into use on 18 October 1936, replacing six previous boxes. Within the box were three signal sub-frames: one for the suburban Platforms 1-4, another for the main-line Platforms 5-15, and the third for the Windsor and Reading line Platforms 16-21 in the 'North' station. In total there were 309 miniature levers and 16 train describers, while four track diagrams covered all lines between Waterloo and Vauxhall. The interior of the box is illustrated at 1137 on Friday 25 February 1977.

Above: **WATERLOO** Also photographed from the signal box on the same day, but with the camera moved to a slightly different angle to include most of the main-line station, in the foreground we see a Class 33 diesel-electric locomotive reversing into Platform 14 to couple up and form the next service to Exeter St David's; the '62' headcode is displayed ready for the journey. The 4TC unit in the centre of the photograph forms part of a service from Weymouth and Bournemouth; propelled by the high-horsepower 4REP units between Waterloo and Bournemouth, and powered by push-pull-fitted Class 33 diesel-electric locomotives between Bournemouth and Weymouth, these trailer units were associated with that line between 1967 and 1988, when electrification was completed to Weymouth. As carriages they gave very good service – they had not been new in 1967 but had been converted from former locomotive-hauled BR Standard Mark 1 stock dating from the 1950s.

...and down the line to Clapham

QUEEN'S ROAD BATTERSEA station, situated between Vauxhall and Clapham Junction, was opened by the LSWR on 1 November 1877; almost 100 years later Ray Ruffell took this photograph from the 1426 Waterloo to Hampton Court service on Monday 31 January 1977. Crossing the overbridge in the centre of the photograph is a two-car train forming a South London Line service between London Bridge and Victoria. The rolling stock is of some interest; it was originally a 2HAP unit dating from 1957 but built on the reclaimed underframes of withdrawn 2NOL stock and therefore given Southern Railway Bulleid-style bodywork. In 1976 the 36 units of this type had been transferred to Selhurst and made 2nd Class only for use on suburban duties (the former 1st Class compartments in the driving trailers were obviously the most popular part of the train with customers until they were given 2nd Class seating on overhaul). These units were progressively withdrawn in the early 1980s and all had been taken out of service by May 1983. Queen's Road Battersea station was subsequently renamed Queenstown Road Battersea from 12 May 1980. Current platform signage and some recent system maps omit the Battersea suffix; conversely, above the main entrance to the premises from the street 'LSWR Queen's Road Station' is still shown in large letters.

Above: **CLAPHAM** Years before the coming of the railway, this part of London was rural in character, and was known for the growing of lavender – this is still remembered in the nearby street name Lavender Hill. The title was also used for the 1951 Ealing Studios film *The Lavender Hill Mob*, which starred Alec Guinness and Stanley Holloway with Sid James and Alfie Bass and told of a gold bullion robbery that led to a number of amusing situations. By the 20th century the area was, of course, the home to one of the busiest stretches of railway in Europe, carrying around 2,000 trains each day.

On Wednesday 5 October 1977 Ray Ruffell photographed an identified Class 33 diesel-electric locomotive at the head of a long train of empty wagons from the Allington stone terminal.

Below left: **CLAPHAM JUNCTION** The 4VEP units, first introduced in 1967, were something of a hybrid between suburban and main-line stock. They were gangwayed throughout and included 1st Class compartments, but the open saloon 2nd Class accommodation consisted of high-density 3+2 seating, with a slam door to each seating bay and offering no greater comfort than a SUB or EPB unit. Conceived for main-line stopping services, their high capacity also made them very useful crowd-clearers for summer relief trains. No 7825 was one of a batch of 4VEP units built in 1972, and was photographed at Clapham Junction on Tuesday 17 May 1977 operating a semi-fast service from Farnham to Waterloo via Earlsfield.

Above right: **CLAPHAM JUNCTION** When the Waterloo-Bournemouth line was electrified in 1967, there was a need for some additional more powerful electro-diesel locomotives for such workings as ocean liner express trains to Southampton Docks. The 24 electric locomotives that had been built for the Kent Coast electrification schemes in the late 1950s were found to be a generous provision for the traffic on offer by the mid-1960s, so ten locomotives from this batch were withdrawn for conversion to electro-diesels at British Railways Crewe Works. One such locomotive was No 74001, which had entered traffic as E5015 in February 1960; withdrawn for conversion to electro-diesel in August 1966, it did not re-enter traffic until February 1968 as E6101, later being renumbered 74001 under the TOPS scheme. When photographed on Tuesday 17 May arriving at Clapham Yard with empty stock from a boat train, its days were numbered; it was withdrawn in December.

...and down the line to Clapham

Below: **CLAPHAM YARD** The extensive station at Clapham Junction is effectively triangular in shape, as the lines from Waterloo to Barnes, Richmond and Windsor, etc, continue due west, while the platforms serving the lines towards Woking and the lines from Victoria to Selhurst, etc, follow a more south-westerly alignment. Clapham Yard lies in between the two sections of the station, with sidings for both electric multiple units and locomotive-hauled stock, as illustrated in this photograph taken on Friday 20 May 1977. The two EMUs closest to the camera are both from the early 1970s build of 4CIG units; No 7354 on the right was intended for the Waterloo-Portsmouth line and was allocated to Fratton depot, while No 7383 was provided to the Waterloo-Reading route and was allocated to Wimbledon.

Below: **CLAPHAM JUNCTION** This inspection saloon, powered by Class 33/1 No 33102, was an interesting visitor to Clapham Junction on Tuesday 17 May. It had been built as a Kitchen Car by the LMS at Derby in 1938 and served in that role for 20 years before being converted for departmental use

as an inspection and observation saloon in 1958. The carriage was only 50 feet long as built, and observation windows replaced the former gangwayed ends. When photographed the carriage was being used a guards' route-learning coach. Class 33/1 No 33102 had entered traffic in June 1960 as D6513; adapted for push-pull operation in October 1967, this locomotive was preserved following withdrawal in November 1992 and is currently located on the Churnet Valley Railway.

Below left: **CLAPHAM YARD** Ray Ruffell's daughter, Margaret, accompanied him on many photographic excursions, and was sometimes able to see railway life behind the scenes. On Wednesday 30 March 1977 the then eight-year-old Margaret was photographed by her father in the driving seat of a 4SUB unit. With hand outstretched to the master controller, she certainly is concentrating on the view ahead. The functional simplicity of the driver's accommodation on these late-1940s units is very apparent. Nonetheless these rugged and reliable trains served the Southern Region very well until the last was withdrawn from service in September 1983.

1977 Arrivals & Departures

Births

Michelle Behennah	Model	7 January
Orlando Bloom	Actor	13 January
Hayley Tamaddon	Actress	24 January
Ben Ainslie	Competitive sailor	5 February
Colin Murray	Radio DJ	10 March
Adrian Morely	Rugby League footballer	10 May
Samantha Morton	Actress	13 May
Rachael Stirling	Actress	30 May
Joel Ross	Radio DJ	31 May
Angela Beesley	Co-founder of Wikia	3 August
Danny Griffin	Footballer	10 August
Gavin Meadows	Freestyle swimmer	8 September
Alistair Griffin	Singer/songwriter	1 November
Kavana (Anthony Kavanagh)	Singer	4 November
Peter Phillips	Son of HRH The Princess Royal	15 November
Paul McVeigh	Footballer	6 December
Matt Baker	Television presenter	23 December

Deaths

Anthony Eden	Politician	(b1897)	14 January
Peter Finch	Actor	(b1916)	14 January
Anthony Crossland	Politician	(b1918)	19 February
Madeline Dring	Composer/actress	(b1923)	26 March
Stephen Boyd	Actor	(b1931)	2 June
Lady Olave Baden-Powell	Chief Girl Guide	(b1889)	25 June
Henry Williamson	Writer	(b1895)	13 August
Edward Sinclair	Actor	(b1914)	29 August
Leopold Stokowski	Musician	(b1882)	13 September
Marc Bolan	Musician	(b1947)	16 September
Terence Rattigan	Playwright	(b1911)	30 November
Charlie Chaplin	Actor	(b1889)	25 December

The Great Northern route from King's Cross

Right: **KING'S CROSS** Eight-year-old Margaret Ruffell is clearly pleased to be photographed beside Class 55 'Deltic' No 55007 *Pinza* on Wednesday 26 October 1977 – seeing her happy smile and the open doorway, I suspect she may have just been invited to have a quick look in the cab. *Pinza* had entered traffic in June 1961 as D9007, and remained in service with British Rail until December 1981. Platform staff are loading the front van before the train departs as the 0900 service to York. The station at King's Cross opened in 1852 and was designed by Lewis Cubitt for the Great Northern Railway; it effectively consisted of two parallel arch-roofed train sheds, each 800 feet long and 105 feet wide. The simple effectiveness of Cubitt's design is well illustrated in the photograph, which nicely captures the atmosphere of King's Cross as it was in the late 1970s.

Right: **FINSBURY PARK DEPOT** Built on the site of the old Clarence Yard, Finsbury Park Traction Maintenance Depot was British Railways' first purpose-built main-line diesel depot, and came into use in April 1960. Standing outside the depot on Thursday 3 March 1977 is Class 55 'Deltic' locomotive No 55003 *Meld*; new in March 1961 as No D9003, this locomotive was withdrawn in December 1980. The powerful stud of 22 'Deltic' locomotives were the mainstay of express services on the East Coast Main Line from King's Cross to York, Newcastle and Edinburgh, and also to Leeds, until they were replaced by the InterCity 125 High Speed Trains in 1978.

The Great Northern route from King's Cross

Above: **FINSBURY PARK** Although the 'Deltics' worked the majority of the express services on the East Coast Main Line in 1977, the somewhat lower-powered Class 47 locomotives also did good work on these services, as illustrated by an unidentified member of the class near journey's end as it hurries through Finsbury Park with a London-bound express. Notice also the train of BR Standard Mark 1 stock on the left.

FINSBURY PARK The electrified service on the old Great Northern inner suburban lines came into operation from 8 November 1976. To provide the service a total of 64 three-car Class 313 electric multiple units were built by the BR Workshops at York. These were dual-voltage units, being fitted with pantographs for operation at 25kV AC from overhead wires, and pick-up shoes for use on 750V DC from a third rail. As part of the electrification scheme the line was linked to the Underground line between Drayton Park and Moorgate, which until October 1975 had run as a separate branch of London Transport's Northern Line. Changeover from AC to DC operation is made at Drayton Park station, where all trains must stop. Still looking shiny and new, Class 313 unit No 313006 heads a six-car Moorgate-bound train into Finsbury Park station on Thursday 3 March 1977.

FINSBURY PARK Between 1932 and 1972 Pullman car *Doris* was formed in 5BEL electric multiple unit No 3051 and plied between London Victoria and Brighton in the 'Brighton Belle'. With the withdrawal of the 'Belle' in 1972, *Doris* was sold to City Industrial Limited (shopfitters), and for 34 years was stabled here in the former milk dock on the west side of Finsbury Park station, where she was photographed on Thursday 3 March 1977. She left this North London location in 2006 and moved to the Bluebell Railway in Sussex; subsequently she has moved again to become part of the exciting project to restore a 5BEL unit to working condition. The new Class 313 unit in the foreground looks quite utilitarian compared with the distinguished veteran *Doris*, complete with curtains and the characteristic Pullman table lamps.

The Great Northern route from King's Cross

YORK Replacing a former terminus station that dated from 1841, where the need to reverse through trains in and out was a serious impediment, the present station at York dates from 1877. One of the most attractive and graceful large stations, it is situated on a curve with the platforms within the main structure sheltered by overall span roofs. Looking north from the footbridge on Wednesday 26 October 1977, Class 47 diesel-electric No 47478 brings a rake of air-conditioned stock into the main up platform forming a Newcastle to London King's Cross working. Built at British Railways Crewe Works and entering traffic in July 1964 as D1608, this locomotive remained in service for over 41 years, being withdrawn in December 2005.

Derailment at Clink Road Junction

CLINK ROAD JUNCTION The derailment of a stone train from Whatley Quarry, Frome, in April 1977 caused serious damage to both the track and the stock of the train. The main line from London to the West Country and the route from Westbury to Weymouth were blocked, and the Mendip stone traffic was ensnared; work to restore services went ahead very quickly. The damaged wagons were moved to the trackside to be recovered at a later date. To get trains running again as soon as possible the trailing connection between the main line and the Frome loop was temporarily taken out, allowing a resumption of services, albeit that all up trains had to proceed via Frome. Brian Jackson took this photograph looking west at Clink Road Junction on Sunday 3 April showing the work in progress. *Brian Jackson*

Left: **CLINK ROAD JUNCTION** signal box, which had come into use from 2 January 1933, is seen in this photograph looking east on the same day, with work to restore train services proceeding apace. Damage to the track and the wagons had been severe and, although not seen in the photograph, a considerable number of upturned wagons lay beyond the bridge. Clink Road Junction signal box was closed from 7 October 1984 when the area came under the control of Westbury panel, and the structure was demolished shortly afterwards. *Brian Jackson*

Right: **WESTBURY** The derailment at Clink Road Junction required the attendance of specialist engineers' equipment at the site. Photographed at Westbury after their work was complete is No PWM650 with a track-panel-laying machine. Operated by the Civil Engineer's Department, this locomotive dated from 1953 and was one of five such machines built by Ruston & Hornsby of Lincoln between 1952 and 1959. Preserved after withdrawal, at the time of writing PWM650 is located at the Lincolnshire Wolds Railway. *Brian Jackson*

Derailment at Clink Road Junction

Above: **WESTBURY** Also at Westbury on Sunday 3 April 1977 was this former Great Western Railway 'Iron Mink' van No TDW105781. It had been built as a Gunpowder van in 1939 from a basic design that dated back to the end of the 19th century. No doubt because of their hazardous loads, such Gunpowder vans had only been permitted to carry 7 tons although, not being fitted with screw couplings or vacuum brakes, they had been worked as unfitted freight stock. *Brian Jackson*

Above right and right: **WESTBURY** Also attending, and seen here waiting to return to Bristol, was TDW19, one of four 45-ton cranes acquired by the Great Western Railway in 1939 as part of a Government scheme in preparation for hostilities. Although classified as breakdown cranes – which was their prime purpose – they were always kept in readiness to deal with derailments and other incidents. They were also used for replacing bridges and other heavy structures when required. Their lifting capacity was higher than previous rail-mounted cranes, although the 45-ton lift was only possible under ideal conditions with a fully raised jib, and blocking and stabilisers in position.

Not often seen in close-up by the general public, the mechanical detail of these machines was fascinating – perhaps especially to boys who were brought up with Meccano, that marvellous construction kit based on engineering principles. Several large railway breakdown cranes have been preserved and can be seen on heritage railways. *Brian Jackson*

On the Isle of Wight

RYDE PIER HEAD This was the delightful scene that greeted visitors to the Isle of Wight in 1977 after they had disembarked from the ferry at Ryde. When the line had been electrified ten years earlier, Platform 2 had been extended across a former running line to allow a train to terminate on a line with a platform on both sides; it could then load from one side while simultaneously unloading from the other. The alterations to the station can be clearly seen in the photograph – it is a pity that the canopy over Platforms 2 and 3 was not similarly extended. Both of the former London Transport driving motor cars seen here on Saturday 26 March were built by the Metropolitan Carriage & Wagon Company in 1934; nearest to the camera car No S10S was the 'spare' motor car – which the numbers in the cab window show was being temporarily used to power 3TIS unit No 034 – while car No S2S forms the 'A' end power car of 4VEC unit No 043.

RYDE PIER It is not possible to use normal full-size rolling stock on the Isle of Wight system owing to restricted clearances in the tunnel between Ryde Esplanade and Ryde St John's Road, so when the remaining line between Ryde Pier Head and Shanklin was electrified in 1967 superannuated tube stock was adapted for the line. For those that remembered the trains carrying crush loads beneath the streets of London, the sight of these veterans running along Ryde Pier was slightly surreal. Here a train approaches Ryde Esplanade station on Monday 27 June 1977. When these trains were introduced to the Isle of Wight, platform levels were adjusted by raising the tracks at all locations except Ryde Esplanade, where the platforms were lowered.
Brian Jackson

RYDE ESPLANADE Viewed from the footbridge that provides a pedestrian link between the bus station and the hovercraft terminal, two trains formed of former London Underground stock are seen in Ryde Esplanade station. The driving motor car on the Shanklin end of 3TIS unit No 034 seen on the left was built by the Metropolitan Carriage & Wagon Company in 1931. Ryde Esplanade had long been an important terminal point for Southern Vectis buses, and when the station was rebuilt in the early 1970s the opportunity was taken to also provide a purpose-built bus station with eight saw-tooth-type departure bays. Ryde bus station was opened on 25 May 1974, and the very convenient interchange between buses and trains is nicely illustrated in this photograph taken just over three years later on Monday 27 June 1977. *Brian Jackson*

RYDE ST JOHN'S ROAD Being separate from the mainland and operated by elderly and non-standard equipment, the Isle of Wight lines had always been largely self-sufficient in terms of maintenance over the years. In the latter days of steam operation, the small works at Ryde St John's Road had performed miracles to keep the locomotives and rolling stock in good running condition despite much of it being 60 or more years old. From 1967 the resourceful and dedicated band of engineers ably turned their hands to looking after the former Underground stock. Two carriages are seen awaiting attention on that same June day; that nearest the camera had originally entered service with London Transport in 1925. *Brian Jackson*

RYDE ST JOHN'S ROAD While in service on the Isle of Wight, the former London Underground 'Standard' stock, which dated from 1923 to 1934, was marshalled into four-car (4VEC) and three-car (3TIS) sets. When these were joined to make a seven-car train it became a VECTIS – Vectis being the Roman name for the Isle of Wight. Such a seven-car VECTIS formation was photographed approaching Ryde St John's Road on Monday 27 June 1977 forming a service from Shanklin to Ryde Pier Head. Like most of the equipment used on the island's railways, Ryde St John's Road signal box, seen on the right, was second-hand. It had originated with the South Eastern & Chatham Railway, and stood at Waterloo Junction until being moved here in 1928. In the 21st century it is the sole surviving signal box controlling the entire 8.5-mile electrified line. *Brian Jackson*

BRADING Opened in 1864, the station at Brading was the junction for the branch to St Helens and Bembridge from 1882 until 1953. While the line from Ryde to Shanklin had been electrified in 1967, little had been done to Brading station ten years later; at that time it was still gas-lit and a Southern Railway running-in board was in evidence. Electric lighting was finally installed at Brading in 1986, but unfortunately the line through the station was singled in October 1988; this means that it is no longer possible to photograph two trains passing at this location, and moreover restricts the service headway on the line to multiples of 20 minutes (for example, a service of three trains per hour can run every 20 minutes, but two trains per hour must be at 20/40-minute intervals rather than every half-hour). On Saturday 26 March 1977 the front cab of a train for Ryde can be seen in the right foreground as 4VEC unit No 041 approaches the down platform with a train for Shanklin. The leading car of unit No 041 dates from 1931, the two centre cars from 1923, and the rear car from 1928.

SHANKLIN 3TIS unit No 031 brings up the rear of a train departing from Shanklin for Ryde on Monday 27 June 1977; the upper-quadrant starting signal, economically mounted on old rail, has already dropped back to the 'on' position. Notice the red disc in lieu of an oil tail lamp on the rear of the train; this was a practice only employed on the Isle of Wight. *Brian Jackson*

SHANKLIN Opened in 1862, Shanklin has been the southern terminus of the line from Ryde since the extension to Ventnor was closed in 1966. By the time this photograph was taken on Saturday 26 March 1977 only the former down platform was regularly in use, although it can be seen that both platform lines had been electrified. The former up platform on the right was used during the peak summer period during the first two years of electric services, but was not used for passenger trains after the 1968 season, and the passenger subway linking the platforms was closed. The platform canopy on the old up platform had been removed when this photograph was taken, although the signal box remained; this has also since been demolished and the track through the former up platform has been lifted. Eight-year-old Margaret Ruffell stands beside the cab of the 'A' end motor car of 4VEC unit No 043, a car that had entered service on the London Underground's Piccadilly Line in 1934.

Catch it while you can: 'The Corkscrew Shuttle'

WIMBORNE The original railway route between Southampton and Dorchester ran via Ringwood and Wimborne and was opened by the Southampton & Dorchester Railway Company in 1847; the company was amalgamated into the LSWR the following year. The line had been promoted by Wimborne solicitor Charles Castleman, and given the indirect route that it followed between Southampton and Dorchester it was soon referred to as 'Castleman's Corkscrew'. A more direct route via Sway, Bournemouth and Poole to Hamworthy and Dorchester was fully completed in 1893; the original route then became a secondary line, and was referred to by local railwaymen as 'the old road'. Although useful as a diversionary route, and also used by summer Saturday extra trains to and from London Waterloo right through until the 1963 summer season, the 'old road' was closed to passengers in May 1964. Closure to goods traffic followed in sections, until by early 1977 only the section between Poole and Wimborne remained, and this was scheduled for closure in May of that year. On Sunday 1 May the Lea Valley Railway Club ran 'The Corkscrew

Catch it while you can: 'The Corkscrew Shuttle'

Shuttle', which operated three round trips between Bournemouth, Poole and Wimborne. The train, photographed at Wimborne station, consisted of Class 33 diesel-electric locomotive No 33107 and two 4TC units. New in September 1960 as D6520, and converted for push-pull operation in May 1967, No 33107 remained in service with British Rail until May 1989.

Two days after this photograph was taken, Class 33 diesel-electric No 33012 hauled the last ever freight train over the line, which carried a handwritten headboard 'The last train from Wimborne, 3 May 1977'. By the summer of 1978 track-lifting was completed and the 'old road' was no more. In the 21st century some sections of the former trackbed between Ringwood and Upton are used as a footpath and cycleway, which is very appropriately called the Castleman Trailway. *Brian Jackson*

West from Paddington

Above: **PADDINGTON** Designed by Isambard Kingdom Brunel and Sir Matthew Digby Wyatt, the present terminus at London Paddington dates from 1854 and replaces an earlier temporary terminus that had opened in 1838. Although subsequently extended and in places rebuilt – notably during the 1930s – Brunel and Wyatt would still recognise the station in the 21st century. InterCity 125 High Speed Trains had been introduced on the Paddington to Bristol and South Wales routes from 1976; the timetable applying from 4 October that year included 11 trains each way between Paddington and Swansea and five each way between Paddington and Bristol scheduled for 125mph running along the authorised sections of track. Illustrating the new image at this historic station, five InterCity 125 HSTs can be seen at Paddington on Friday 26 August 1977.

Below: **READING** Until September 1965 Southern Region trains serving Reading from Waterloo or from Tonbridge had run into a separate terminus station adjacent to the Western Region's Reading General station. The Southern station was then closed and the Waterloo and Tonbridge services were diverted into a new platform, numbered 4a, at Reading General; this was the only platform in the Western Region station to be equipped for third rail electric trains. In due course the new platform, which could accommodate trains up to eight carriages in length, was found to be insufficient, so a further additional platform, numbered 4b and also electrified, was opened along its outer edge in 1975. On Tuesday 28 June 1977 4CIG unit No 7383, dating from the early 1970s, stands at Platform 4b with a Waterloo service, while 'Tadpole' diesel-electric unit No 1204 stand at Platform 4a waiting to depart for Tonbridge via Guildford. The modern canopy over Platforms 4a and 4b contrasts with the style of the rest of the station. On the extreme left of the photograph the car park just visible beside the 4CIG unit occupies the site of the former Southern station. Reading station was being extensively rebuilt and enlarged in 2012-13.

Top: **READING** Seen from Platform 4a on Monday 5 September, Class 31 diesel-electric locomotives Nos 31414 and 31416 are double-heading an up express bound for Paddington. The Class 31s were built by Brush Traction of Loughborough and were originally equipped with Mirrlees engines, but these were progressively replaced by English Electric units from 1964 onwards. Leading the formation seen here, No 31414 entered traffic in September 1961 as D5842; subsequently withdrawn in February 1999, it has been preserved and at the time of writing can be seen at the Ecclesbourne Valley Railway in Derbyshire. The second locomotive, No 31416, was new in May 1962 and was scrapped following withdrawal in October 1995. The leading carriage of the train is British Railways Standard Mark 2b side corridor 1st (FK) No W13513, which was new in 1969.

Middle: **READING** A Stratford to Millbrook Freightliner train, photographed from Platform 4a passing through Reading station on Wednesday 29 June, is powered by Class 47 diesel-electric locomotive No 47444. Built at British Railways Crewe Works and originally numbered D1560, this locomotive was in traffic with British Rail from March 1964 until November 1990. Having travelled from the Stratford Freightliner depot via the North London Line and Acton Wells Junction to Reading, the working will continue via Mortimer and Basingstoke to the Freightliner terminal at Millbrook, just west of Southampton Central. Notice that the electrified line serving Platform 4a in the foreground is entirely separate from the through Western Region lines.

Bottom: **READING** The Class 50 diesel-electric locomotives were built by English Electric at the Vulcan Foundry to power express passenger trains between Crewe and Glasgow on the West Coast Main Line. When the electrification was completed through to Glasgow and came into operation from 6 May 1974, it released the Class 50s to be transferred to the Western Region – which in due course allowed the withdrawal of the non-standard diesel-hydraulic 'Western' Class. On Saturday 23 April 1977 No 50039 comes into Reading station with a down working from London Paddington. Entering traffic as D439 in September 1968, this locomotive was subsequently named *Implacable* in June 1978 and was withdrawn in June 1989. Notice that the locomotive number has also been displayed in the headcode box.

At Platform 5 power car No 43037 at the head of InterCity 125 High Speed Train No 253 018, new in November 1976, awaits departure for the final sprint to Paddington.

1977 Happenings (2)

READING When the InterCity 125 HSTs were first introduced on the Western Region in 1976, lavish provision was made for on-train catering. Each unit included a TRUK – a Kitchen Car that included 24 seats for dining passengers, which were of 1st Class configuration but could be used by both 1st and 2nd Class passengers while taking a meal during their journey. There was also a TRSB in each unit, which provided a counter service of drinks and snacks. It soon became clear that the TRUK restaurant cars were little used apart from at breakfast time; possibly owing to the relatively short journey times now achieved between London and Bristol/South Wales, passenger take-up for luncheon or dinner was small. In the event only 20 of the TRUK restaurant cars were built, the later-constructed units having just one catering car – the compromise TRUB. TRUK Restaurant Car No W40510 is seen in an up train at Reading on Tuesday 28 June 1977 while still allocated to its originally intended duties; this carriage was later adapted at British Rail Derby Litchurch Lane Works for use in locomotive-hauled trains, and served as a catering car on the West Coast Main Line between London Euston and Glasgow.

EXETER ST DAVID'S is the location of this Wednesday 21 September 1977 photograph of Class 25 diesel-electric locomotive No 25080, one of a class of 327 built between 1961 and 1967. In the West Country the Class 25s took over the duties that had been performed by the less successful North British 'Baby Warship' diesel-hydraulics numbered in the D63XX series, a class of 59 locomotives built between 1959 and 1962 that had all been withdrawn by the end of 1972. Seen awaiting the next turn of duty, No 25080 was built at British Railways Darlington Works and entered traffic in October 1963 as D5230; it was subsequently withdrawn in September 1985. *Brian Jackson*

July
- Don Revie resigns after three years as manager of England national football team – and quickly accepts offer to become manager of United Arab Emirates football team.
- Tommy Docherty is dismissed as manager of Manchester United – his replacement is Dave Sexton from Queen's Park Rangers.

August
- Stage Three voluntary one-year pay restraint introduced by Government.
- RMS *Windsor Castle* makes Union Castle Line's final passenger/mail voyage from Southampton to Cape Town.
- Ron Greenwood, general manager of West Ham United, appointed temporary manager of England national football team.
- New-style smaller pound note is introduced.

September
- Figures indicate that for first time total sales of foreign cars have exceeded those for British models on home market.
- Freddie Laker launches 'Skytrain' airline – charging £59 from Gatwick to New York compared with normal fare of £186.

West from Paddington

October
- Undertakers go on strike in London.
- Former Liberal leader Jeremy Thorpe denies allegations of attempted murder.

November
- National strike by firefighters starts; they seek a 30% wage rise.
- HRH Princess Anne gives birth to son, making Her Majesty the Queen a grandmother for first time.
- British Airways starts regular supersonic Concorde service between London and New York.

December
- Ron Greenwood confirmed as manager of England national football team.
- Queen opens extension of London Underground Piccadilly Line from Hatton Cross (terminus since 1975) to Heathrow Central, bringing direct Underground link to London Airport.

Right: **PENZANCE** On a wet day in 1977 two trains headed by Class 50 diesel-electric locomotives await departure from Penzance. Opened by the West Cornwall Railway in 1852, the station was rebuilt by the Great Western Railway in 1880 and 1939, although the rather cramped location effectively on a ledge between Chyandour Cliff and the sea made expansion difficult. This terminus is 305.25 miles from London Paddington, and passengers arriving here are greeted by a large stone slab near the end of Platform 4 that carries the message 'Welcome to Penzance', written in both English and Cornish. This photograph was taken looking over the wall from Chyandour Cliff, a great place to watch the trains, with part of the town and the sea in the background. *Brian Jackson*

Right: **PENZANCE** Standing out against a stormy sky, and with Mounts Bay in the background, two starting signals at Penzance station are seen together with a modern concrete lamp post. Over the years the railway scene has evolved through a gradual modernisation process. Whereas the Southern Railway tended to use old rail to supersede wooden and steel lattice signal posts, the Great Western Railway tended to use tubular steel posts – which in recent years have become the standard for the majority of electric signals. The state of progress in Penzance in 1977 is shown here. *Brian Jackson*

London's Underground

Below: **TOWER HILL** station on the District Line was opened in February 1967. The former Tower Hill station had been located about 100 yards further west, and had been known as Mark Lane until 1946. The 1967 station occupies the site of the original Tower of London station, which was only in use for two years from 1882 until replaced by Mark Lane in 1884. One of the reasons for the 1967 rebuild was to move the terminus for short workings on the District Line further east from Mansion House; the former westbound through track was made a terminating and reversing point, with a new westbound through track being provided on the other side of a wide island westbound platform. The R stock train photographed on Wednesday 24 August 1977 has terminated at Tower Hill and is waiting to run to Ealing Broadway. The District Line R stock consisted of a mixture of new cars built between 1949 and 1959 and rebuilt cars dating from 1938-40. Nearest to the camera, car No 22606 entered service in December 1940 as a trailer car, was rebuilt and converted to a driving motor car for the R stock programme in 1950, and remained in service with London Transport until September 1982.

Above: **WIMBLEDON PARK** Immediately south of Wimbledon Park station the District Line runs beside British Rail's Wimbledon Park sidings. A train formed of R stock bound for Wimbledon is seen here in April 1977; the Southern Region suburban train on the right is a BR Standard 2HAP unit that had temporarily been downgraded to 2nd Class only for suburban duties. Notice that the front carriage of the R stock train has four separate windows between the sets of double doors, indicating that it is one of the rebuilt cars from 1938-40; the newly built post-war stock had two wider windows in this position, as seen on the second and third cars of this train.

MORDEN Opened in 1926 and designed by Charles Holden, Morden station is the southern terminus of the Northern Line. A train of 1959 stock, originally built for the Piccadilly Line and transferred to the Northern Line in 1975, enters the station on Sunday 20 March 1977. This train has just travelled through what in 1977 was the world's longest continuous railway tunnel – 17.25 miles from East Finchley to Morden via Bank, including 24 stations and three junctions. Notice the timber-framed roundel-style station name board on the platform; this is the 1926 original.

MORDEN Another view of Morden station on the same day shows part of the steel-trussed glazed roof that covers much of the platform area. The station is situated in a cutting and the running lines northwards almost at once plunge into tunnel, as can be seen in the background. Further original 1926 station name signs can be seen in this photograph, although the name sign and poster display in front of the clock and closest to the camera is a modern replacement. The line continues a short distance south of Morden station to a depot and stabling sidings. The train seen on the left of this photograph is formed of 1972 stock, which ran in service on the Northern Line until 1999.

HAMMERSMITH When opened in 1874 this was the western terminus of the District Railway, which had been extended from Earls Court; it became a through station three years later when the District was further extended. What was then called the Great Northern, Piccadilly & Brompton Railway also terminated here, in separate platforms on the north side of the station, from 1906. Hammersmith station was rebuilt in 1932, when what had become the Piccadilly Line was also extended further west. It was then that the layout seen here on Friday 26 August 1977 was introduced, with the Piccadilly Line tracks in the centre flanked by the District Line tracks, offering cross-platform interchange between the two lines. The two Piccadilly Line trains contrast the 1973 stock (on the left) with the 1959 stock (on the right); by 1977 the majority of 1959 stock had been transferred to the Northern Line.

ARNOS GROVE, opened in September 1932, was temporarily the terminus of the Piccadilly Line extension north from Finsbury Park. It became a through station when the line was further extended to Oakwood (then called Enfield West) in March 1933, and onwards to Cockfosters in July of that year. The station was designed by Charles Holden and the street-level buildings are well worth seeing as they epitomise 1930s railway architecture and are Grade 2* listed. Two trains of 1973 stock can be seen; that nearest the camera will run via central London to Rayners Lane, and will enter the tube tunnel before the next station at Bounds Green. The lines behind the cable runs on the left of the photograph lead to Arnos Grove sidings, also opened in 1932.

Above: **SOUTHGATE** Although the Piccadilly Line comes out into the open south of Arnos Grove, there is one further short section in tunnel, taking the line beneath a hill at Southgate, before the terminus at Cockfosters, and its southern portal is seen here on Thursday 3 March 1977. Southgate station is within this tunnel section and is well worth a visit. Also designed by Charles Holden, it has a circular ticket hall, while the old-style uplighters survive on the escalators and lower concourse; it is regarded as one of the most significant 1930s public buildings in London, and is Grade 2* listed. Being situated in a relatively short length of tunnel, Southgate is also unique as the only deep-level tube station where it is possible to look along the line and see daylight.

Above right: **COCKFOSTERS** opened in July 1933, and is the terminus of the Piccadilly Line extension from Finsbury Park. It was another station designed by Charles Holden, although in a different style from Arnos Grove or Southgate. Nonetheless, the ticket hall, concourse and platforms have a very spacious feel, as can be seen from the photograph taken on Thursday 3 March 1977, and the station is Grade 2 listed. The train, which will shortly depart for Rayners Lane, is formed of 1973 stock with which the Piccadilly Line was re-equipped in 1975 ready for the subsequent extension of services from Hounslow West to Heathrow Airport; this stock is still in service on the line at the time of writing. Notice the Ford Anglia 105E Super in the car park on the right.

Above: **HAINAULT** In 1903 the Great Eastern Railway opened a loop line linking Woodford with Ilford via Chigwell, Hainault and Newbury Park; at the 1923 Grouping operation passed to the LNER. The 1935-40 London Railway New Works Programme included the extension of London Transport's Central Line from its then terminus at Liverpool Street, including a new tube line from Leytonstone that would surface at Newbury Park, with Central Line trains then operating over the rest of the loop to Hainault and Woodford. Work was quite advanced when the Second World War intervened, and Underground trains reached Hainault in May 1948, the LNER steam service to Ilford having been discontinued the previous November. A new island platform was provided on the west side of Hainault station and the 1940s-style buildings and canopy can be contrasted with the 1903 Great Eastern Railway canopy, which can be seen on the right of the photograph, sheltering the other platform. Notice in the right foreground the combined roundel and lamp standard in concrete, dating from the 1940s. A train of 1962 stock will shortly depart for Ealing Broadway on Thursday 3 November 1977; trains of this type provided the main Central Line service until 1995.

Below right: **CHIGWELL** Underground trains began operating the rest of the route from Hainault to Woodford in November 1948; for operational reasons the tube trains did not run through round the loop, the section between Hainault and Woodford being operated as a separate shuttle service until the 1990s. In 1960 a dozen experimental driving motor cars were delivered to London Transport by Cravens of Sheffield, and 12 trailer carriages dating from 1927-31 were refurbished, including fluorescent lighting and 'silver' external livery, to run with them to make six four-car units. For a short while these ran on the main Central Line, coupled in pairs as three eight-car trains, the intention being to evaluate the design with a view to re-equipping the Central Line with this type. However, replacement of the line's existing stock, some of which dated back to 1923, became so urgent that the decision was taken to perpetuate the general design of the 1959 stock with a few detailed modifications, and this became the 1962 stock, which soon took over the main section of the Central Line. The 1960 stock was allocated to the Hainault-Woodford shuttle, running as four-car units. In 1964 the shuttle service was adapted as a test bed for automatic train operation (ATO), and thus commenced operation in this form four years before the first section of the Victoria Line was opened. A train of 1960 stock, equipped for ATO, is seen at Chigwell station on the same day as the previous picture. The ATO equipment was removed in 1986 as it was life expired; returned to manual operation, the 1960 stock – later painted red and with a single 1938 stock trailer added to give a train length of three cars – was sometimes used on the Central Line shuttle between Epping and Ongar, but this became sporadic as the age of the cars was taking its toll. All of the 1960 stock was withdrawn in 1994 when the service to Ongar ceased.

LEYTONSTONE By the 1970s the 1938 stock on the Bakerloo and Northern lines was beginning to show its age. Transfer of the 1959 stock from the Piccadilly Line to the Northern Line, together with the introduction of the 1972 stock, allowed some of the cars of 1938 stock that were in the worst condition to be withdrawn. Stripped of its bogies and any reusable equipment, and cut in half to fit the road trailer, a former Northern Line 1938 stock driving motor car is being driven along Leytonstone High Road on Thursday 3 November 1977, making its final journey to the scrapyard. Nonetheless, 1938 stock trains survived on the Bakerloo Line until November 1985, while some refurbished 1938 stock ran once again on the Northern Line between September 1986 and May 1988. And the breed is not yet dead – some of the remaining 1938 stock driving motor cars were sold to British Rail after withdrawal, and after conversion and refurbishment they replaced even older (1923-34) former tube trains on the Isle of Wight (see pages 22-25); the 1938 stock trains entered service on the island from 1989 and at the time of writing continue in daily use there at the grand age of 75 years.

TV favourites

Jesus of Nazareth
With Robert Powell in the title role, this two-part film was shown by ITV on Palm Sunday and Easter Day, attracting huge audiences.

Secret Army
This 16-part series was based on true events as it illustrated the work of the Resistance in occupied Europe during the Second World War.

Robin's Nest
A spin-off from the earlier comedy series *Man about the House*, Richard O'Sullivan (as Robin Tripp) was seen running a restaurant with Tessa Wyatt.

All Creatures Great and Small
Based on James Herriot's books, Christopher Timothy, Robert Hardy and Peter Davison starred in this delightful and nostalgic series about a veterinary practice in Yorkshire.

Abigail's Party
Written and directed by Mike Leigh and shown in the 'Play for Today' series, this depiction of a suburban cocktail party exposed the tastelessness and pretensions displayed by some of the so-called aspiring classes, and it was widely acclaimed.

The Krypton Factor
This new game show combined physical challenges such as an assault course with general knowledge and intelligence tests.

It'll Be Alright on the Night
1977 was the first time that we saw Denis Norden present his hilarious selection of fluffs and errors in popular television shows that had been 'rescued' from the cutting-room floor.

Below: **CLAPHAM JUNCTION** Until April 1994 there was a busy Underground line that was not part of the London Transport network. The Waterloo & City Line was opened in August 1898 and was fully absorbed into the London & South Western Railway in 1907. The branch, 1 mile 46 chains long, thus passed to the Southern Railway in 1923 and became part of British Railways with nationalisation in 1948. The original rolling stock served the line for more 40 years, and was replaced by new stock built by English Electric at the Dick, Kerr Works, Preston. This consisted of 12 driving motor and 16 trailer cars, and trains could be made up of various formations up to a maximum of five cars (a driving motor at each end and three trailers); all 28 replacement cars came into service from 28 October 1940. Although day-to-day maintenance was carried out in the depot at Waterloo, from time to time it was necessary for Waterloo & City cars to receive attention at Eastleigh or another Southern Region workshop. In such cases the car was lifted to the surface on an Armstrong hoist by the old North Sidings at Waterloo, then taken over the main-line network between match wagons. One of the 1940 trailer cars is seen being shunted at Clapham Junction on Friday 20 May 1977 while on its way for works attention.

Above: **WIMBLEDON** Gleaming and shiny after a visit to Eastleigh Works, a 1940 driving motor car is being returned to the Waterloo & City Line on Wednesday 7 September 1977. Each driving motor car had two axle-hung 190hp motors; it will be seen that the body frame is upswept over the motor bogie, and there was a step up in the passenger saloon to a slightly higher floor in this section of the car. There was also a small equipment compartment above the motor bogie between the driver's cab and the passenger saloon. The 1940 stock served the Waterloo & City Line extremely well, remaining in service until May 1993 on a line that is a very important commuter route; until the end the ventilation louvres inside the cars carried the wording 'Southern Railway'. The replacement stock subsequently provided for the Waterloo & City Line in 1993 was a continuation from the build of the 1992 stock that replaced the 1962 stock on London Transport's Central Line; this was perhaps appropriate, as the Waterloo & City line itself was absorbed into the London Transport system in April 1994.

Down in Dorset

The RPPR railtour on Sunday 15 May 1977 started from London Paddington and ran via Swindon, Bristol, Westbury and Yeovil to Maiden Newton, where there was a 20-minute stop; as can be seen, the railtour participants seized the opportunity to look around and take photographs. The ten coach formation of BR Standard Mark 1 stock was double-headed by Class 31 diesel-electric locomotives Nos 31416 and 31414 – the same pairing as we saw at Reading on page 28. After departure from Maiden Newton the railtour continued to Weymouth before returning to Yeovil and taking the branch from Witham to Cranmore, in due course returning to Paddington via Westbury and Bedwyn.

The signal box at the end of the down platform, seen in the second photograph, dated from 1921 and replaced an earlier structure. It was closed in May 1988, but happily Maiden Newton station and the line from Weymouth to Yeovil, Westbury and Bristol remains open and is well used by passengers in the 21st century.
Brian Jackson

MAIDEN NEWTON station, opened in January 1857, was on the Great Western line from Yeovil to Weymouth, and while the majority of passenger traffic between London and that resort used the LSWR route from Waterloo, there were also through trains from Paddington to Weymouth (including the Channel Islands Boat Express) via Westbury, Yeovil and Maiden Newton until September 1959. Situated in the heart of the Dorset countryside, Maiden Newton station was also the junction for the Bridport branch until May 1975, when that scenic branch, together with the stations at Toller, Powerstock and Bridport, was closed. The branch trains used a bay platform at the north end of the up platform (out of sight in these photographs). Part of the old branch trackbed close to the station is now a footpath and cycleway.

No 1 records

January
When a Child is Born — Johnny Mathis
Don't Give Up On Us — David Soul

February
Don't Cry For Me Argentina — Julie Covington
When I Need You — Leo Sayer

March
Chanson D'Amour — Manhattan Transfer

April
Knowing Me, Knowing You — Abba

May
Free — Deniece Williams
I Don't Want To Talk About It/
First Cut Is The Deepest — Rod Stewart

June
Lucille — Kenny Rogers
Show You The Way To Go — Jacksons

July
So You Win Again — Hot Chocolate
I Feel Love — Donna Summer

August
Angelo — Brotherhood of Man
Float On — Floaters

September
Way Down — Elvis Presley

October
Silver Lady — David Soul
Yes Sir, I Can Boogie — Baccara

November
The Name of the Game — Abba

December
Mull of Kintyre/Girls' School — Wings

Above: **RADIPOLE** Originally having timber platforms, this halt – just 1 mile from Weymouth station – was opened in 1905, the year that the railway started running buses in the town as an answer to a proposed electric tram system (which did not materialise). In 1946 Radipole Halt was reconstructed with concrete platforms, but it was not until 1977 that the GWR 'pagoda' huts were replaced by

'bus shelter'-type structures. When the halt was photographed on Monday 13 June 1977 the 'pagoda' on the up platform had been demolished – the remains can be seen lying behind the platform – although that on the down platform was still in place. Radipole Halt was closed on 31 December 1983, exactly 50 years after the last GWR motor bus ran in Weymouth. *Brian Jackson*

Above: **WEYMOUTH** These days any irregularities in the track are quickly and accurately detected by special track inspection trains that have the benefit of the latest electronic equipment. Originally on the Great Western Railway this task had been carried out by filling a carriage toilet with whitewash and relying on an employee to flush it when rough riding was detected. This rather hit-and-miss method was developed into the dreaded 'whitewash coach' – detested by the track gangs – fitted with measuring equipment, but still depositing its message as it roamed the rails. Carriage No DW139 was photographed at Weymouth Town station in 1977. Weymouth station was subsequently rebuilt in 1986, and now occupies a much smaller area. *Brian Jackson*

Around Worcester

Right: **WORCESTER FOREGATE STREET** Accessed by steps to the right of this photograph, Foregate Street is the smaller of the two stations serving Worcester, but has a very convenient city-centre location. It is the first station on the line from Worcester to Great Malvern and Hereford, and the bridge carrying the railway over Foregate Street was photographed on Monday 18 July 1977. The double-arrow British Rail logo on the right looks rather utilitarian compared with the GWR crest in the centre of the bridge, which is flanked by crests that are both part of the coat of arms of the City of Worcester. The Latin motto on the left reads 'Civitas in bello et pace fidelis' ('A faithful city in war and peace'), while that on the right declares 'Floreat semper fidelis civitas' ('May the faithful city always flourish'). The bridge is now Grade 2 listed, and has recently undergone restoration work. *Brian Jackson*

Left: **WORCESTER SHRUB HILL** Located on the east of the city, and the larger of Worcester's two stations, Shrub Hill was opened in 1850, although much of the present building dates from 1865 and is to a design by Edward Wilson. Slightly later than the main building, and an absolute gem, is the ladies' room on the up side, which dates from around 1880. Built of cast iron by the local Vulcan Iron Works, the exterior is decorated with classical pilasters and clad in Majolica tiles. This blue and white structure, photographed in July 1977, is a delightful statement of Victorian elegance, and is now Grade 2 listed. *Brian Jackson*

Below: **STOURBRIDGE TOWN** Twenty miles north of the previous photograph, single-car diesel Motor Brake Second No W55012, built by the Gloucester Railway Carriage & Wagon Company in 1958, stands at the somewhat truncated and reduced Stourbridge Town station on Monday 18 July 1977. The short branch between Stourbridge Junction and Stourbridge Town opened on 1 October 1879, with a new station at the latter being constructed in 1901. The lines extending to the goods depot and Stourbridge Basin Goods had been closed in 1965 and provision for passengers reduced to that seen here. Further reduction was to follow in 1980, when a new station was constructed closer to Stourbridge Junction and the site illustrated became a bus station. In the 21st century the remaining 57-chain branch is served by a Parry People Mover providing a high-frequency service that has seen an increase in the numbers of passengers travelling. *Brian Jackson*

Above: **WORCESTER** Viewed from the top of Rainbow Hill Tunnel in July 1977, a Kidderminster-bound diesel multiple unit departs from Worcester. Tunnel Junction signal box is in the foreground, with the line towards Foregate Street station and Hereford curving away to the right. The line ahead that curves round to the left by the motive power depot leads to Shrub Hill station; the spur from Shrub Hill to Foregate Street runs behind the motive power depot. The tower of Worcester Cathedral can be seen on the skyline on the right, while the chimney in the left background is that of a vinegar factory that was once connected to the rail network by a short branch from Shrub Hill. *Brian Jackson*

Southern serendipity

SOUTHAMPTON TERMINUS It was on 11 May 1840 that a special train from London ceremonially opened the through railway route from Nine Elms to Southampton. The London terminus of the line was moved to the present site at Waterloo in 1848, but meanwhile proposals to extend the railway further west from Southampton had materialised in the form of the Southampton & Dorchester Railway, which opened in 1847. Initially trains from London to points west of Southampton had to run to the original terminal station and reverse, but a spur at Northam added in 1858 (over a very sharp curve) eliminated this. The original Southampton station was renamed Southampton Docks that year, and in due course became Southampton Terminus in 1923, a title it retained until closure in September 1966. The LSWR had purchased the Southampton Dock Company in 1892, and railway lines to the Eastern Docks were laid towards the end of the 19th century. This route ran from beside Southampton Terminus station across Canute Road into the docks, and was retained after the Terminus station closed; it still sees occasional use in the 21st century. On Saturday 1 January 1977 Southampton Corporation AEC Regent V No 393 (KOW 901F) passes over the Canute Road crossing, with the Terminus station out of sight to the left, heading for the Floating Bridge (which would close in June 1977 after the opening of the Itchen Bridge). New in 1967, No 393 had a Neepsend body and was in service with Southampton Corporation until 1981.

Although the names and owners of railway companies have changed over the years, often the original name is cast in tablets of stone. This example, mounted in the tympanum of offices in Platform Road, clearly shows that the original occupier of the building was the London & South Western Railway, as owner of Southampton Docks. *Brian Jackson*

Southern serendipity

BASINGSTOKE Looking west from the down side at Basingstoke station on Tuesday 24 May 1977, two Class 20 diesel-electric locomotives are seen coupled nose-to-nose double-heading a freight working towards Battledown. Nos 20042 and 20043 entered service as D8042 and D8043 respectively in November 1959, and were among 228 locomotives of this type built by English Electric between 1957 and 1968. These 1,000hp Type 1 locomotives were built for light freight traffic, but this was in decline by the 1960s and it became common to see Class 20s coupled nose-to-nose in this way to provide a more hefty 2,000hp capable of more substantial freight workings.

WEYBRIDGE Passengers travelling on the local service to Staines from the bay platform at Weybridge on Friday 16 December 1977 may have been surprised at the roomy and comfortable 4TC unit awaiting their custom instead of the usual 2EPB suburban unit. There had been an interruption in the power supply to the third rail on the branch, so the TC unit, powered by Class 74 locomotive No 74005, operating on its 650hp diesel engine, had been drafted in to maintain the service. Originally built at British Railways Doncaster Works as an electric locomotive for the Kent Coast lines, and entering traffic in May 1960 as E5019, it had been withdrawn in 1966 to be converted to electro-diesel – primarily for boat train traffic between Waterloo and Southampton Docks. It re-entered service in this form in March 1968, numbered E6105. Although capable of sparkling performances and high speeds in electric mode when on form, these rebuilds were not regarded as particularly successful and soon gained a reputation for unreliability. This duty was something of a swansong for No 74005; all of the Class 74 electro-diesel rebuilds were withdrawn at the end of December 1977.

Below right: **CHESSINGTON SOUTH** Construction of a branch from Motspur Park that was intended to run to Leatherhead via Tolworth and Chessington was commenced early in 1936. Passenger services had reached Chessington South station in May 1939, but thereafter the Second World War intervened to halt further progress. As a training exercise, in 1941-42 the Royal Engineers constructed an embankment onwards to within 500 yards of the next proposed station at Rushett, but the establishment of the London Green Belt in the post-war period meant that previously planned house-building would no longer take place, so the terminus of the branch has remained at Chessington South. Here all trains use what would have been the down platform on the left, where an EPB formation is seen carrying headcode 18 and forming the 1135 to London Waterloo on Thursday 2 June 1977. On the right, 4CEP unit No 7154 – built in 1960 for the second phase of the Kent Coast electrification scheme – forms a schools charter train, bringing children from Charlton (near Woolwich) to Chessington Zoo. The train has been stabled in the disused up platform while the youngsters enjoy their day out; it will be shunted into the down platform to allow them to board for the return journey, as the footbridge and up-side facilities were never completed. Notice the distinctive 'Chisarc' concrete canopy on the down platform, a feature of all of the stations on this branch.

Right: **HAMPTON COURT** The short branch to Hampton Court was opened in 1849, and the terminal buildings were designed to be in keeping with nearby Hampton Court Palace. The branch was electrified in 1916. The train seen waiting to depart for London Waterloo in April 1977 is formed of 4SUB unit No 4660, which was new in February 1950 and remained in traffic until March 1983. It was one of a small number of 4SUB units that was modified during the 1960s with roller-blind headcodes rather than the old-fashioned stencils employed by the majority of this type of stock.

Southern serendipity

Right: **GUILDFORD** Before the opening of the Channel Tunnel in 1994, through freight traffic between mainland Europe and the UK was worked via the Dunkirk-Dover train ferry. The DB ferry wagon photographed at Guildford on Friday 27 May 1977 has used this link, having travelled from Berne in Switzerland with a cargo of boilers and refrigerators. Dominating the skyline in the background is Guildford Cathedral, the only new Anglican cathedral to be built in Southern England since the Reformation; construction started in 1936, and the new cathedral was finally consecrated on 17 May 1961.

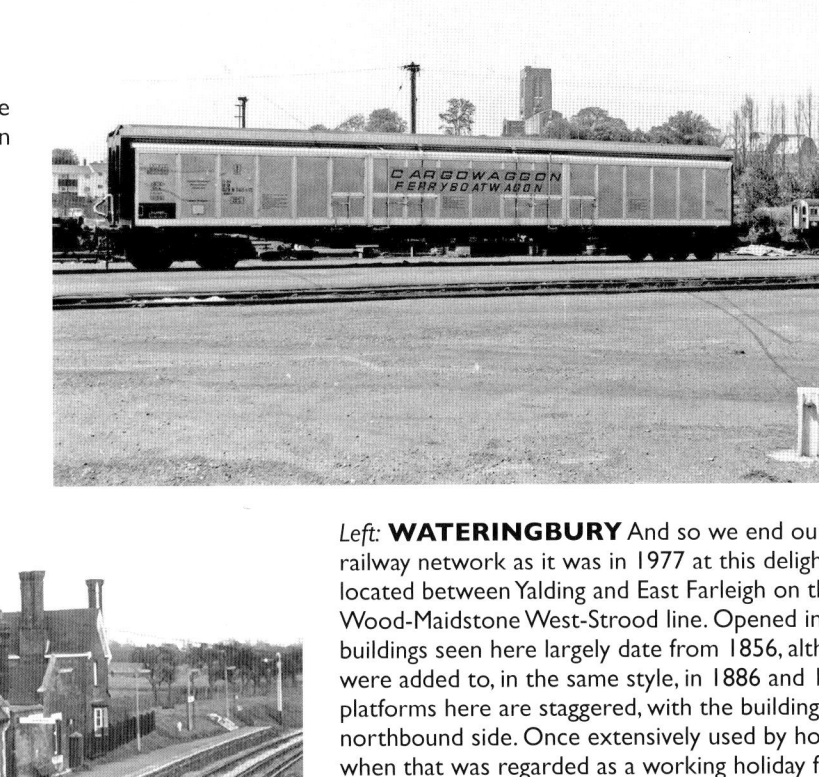

Left: **WATERINGBURY** And so we end our look at the railway network as it was in 1977 at this delightful station, located between Yalding and East Farleigh on the Paddock Wood-Maidstone West-Strood line. Opened in 1844, the buildings seen here largely date from 1856, although they were added to, in the same style, in 1886 and 1889. The platforms here are staggered, with the buildings on the northbound side. Once extensively used by hop-pickers when that was regarded as a working holiday for London folk, it is pleasing that these ornate buildings survive into the 21st century and are now regarded as being among the finest Tudor-style railway buildings in the country. This photograph was taken from the southbound platform on Saturday 2 April 1977. *Brian Jackson*

Acknowledgements

It would not have been possible to produce this book without making use of the photograph collections of Ray Ruffell and Brian Jackson.

The late Ray Ruffell was a railwayman by profession, but his interest in transport went far beyond his day-to-day work. He travelled widely during his off-duty time and created a photographic record of many parts of the railway system during a period when great change was under way. These photographs are now in the safe keeping of The NOSTALGIA Collection, forming a significant part of the company's photographic archive.

Transport historian Brian Jackson also travelled extensively with his camera to record the ever-changing transport scene. Brian has been kind enough to allow me to use many photographs that he took during 1977, and which are credited individually within the book; my warm thanks for his cheerful and willing help.

Many scenes that were everyday and commonplace when Ray or Brian photographed them have now been swept away for ever, and the memories captured on film, precious at the time, are now beyond price.

I would like to say a sincere thank you to the team at The NOSTALGIA Collection for inviting me to write this book. The cheerful and willing help I have received from Peter Townsend, Dave Walshaw and Will Adams has been very much appreciated, and I feel deeply honoured to work with such kind people.

I hope you have enjoyed this look back at 1977 and that you will want to sample more years in the 'Railways & Recollections' series.

Index

General
4TC coaching stock 12, 26, 45
Breakdown train (ex-GWR) 21
Inspection Saloon 15
'Iron Mink' ex-GWR Gunpowder van 21
Mark 2 coaching stock 9
Pullman car *Doris* 18
Silver Jubilee Fleet Review 5-6
Track testing car 41
Waterloo & City Line 38

Locations
Arnos Grove 34
Basingstoke 45
Brading 25
Chessington South 46
Chigwell 36
Clapham Junction 14-15, 38
Clink Road Junction 19-20
Cockfosters 35
Doncaster 4
Exeter St David's 30
Finsbury Park 17-18; depot 16
Guildford 47
Hainault 36
Hammersmith 34
Hampton Court 46
King's Cross 16
Maiden Newton 39
Morden 33
Paddington 28
Penzance 31
Portsmouth Harbour 1, 5
Queen's Road Battersea 13
Radipole 40
Reading 28-30
Ryde Esplanade 23; Pier Head 22; St John's Road 23-24
Sandhurst 48
Shanklin 25-26
Southampton Terminus 44
Southgate 35
Stourbridge Town 43
Tower Hill 32
Wateringbury 47
Waterloo 7-12; control office 8; signal box 12
Westbury 20-21
Weybridge 45
Weymouth 40-41
Wimbledon 38
Wimbledon Park 32
Wimborne 26-27
Worcester 42-43
York 19

Locomotives, diesel
Class 20 45
Class 25 30
Class 31 29, 39
Class 33 12, 14, 15, 26, 40
Class 47 1, 9, 17, 19, 29
Class 50 29, 31
Class 55 'Deltic' 16-17
PWM650 (0-6-0 shunter) 20

Locomotives, electro-diesel
Class 74 14, 45

London Underground
1938 stock 37
1959 stock 33, 34
1960 stock 36
1962 stock 36
1972 stock 33
1973 stock 34, 35
R stock 32

Multiple units, diesel
Class 253 (InterCity 125 HST) 28-30
Single-car 43

Multiple units, electric
2EPB 10
2HAP 13, 32
3TIS 22, 23, 24, 25
4BEP 5
4CEP 46
4CIG 11, 15, 28
4SUB 10, 15, 46
4VEC 22, 24-26
4VEP 14
Class 313 18
'Tadpole' 28